CAPITAL FLIGHT:

Theory, Measurement, and Policy Issues

Rudiger Dornbusch

Massachusetts Institute of Technology

An Occasional Paper
of the IDB

Washington, D.C.

Capital Flight:
Theory, Measurement, and Policy Issues

Occasional Paper No. 2

ISBN: 0-940602-31-8

Available from:
Inter-American Development Bank
1300 New York Ave., N.W.
Washington, D.C. 20577

Exchange:
Library
Inter-American Development Bank

FOREWORD

During the debt crisis of the 1980s, international bankers have often justified their reluctance to lend to Latin America by pointing out that it is not logical to ask them to invest in the region while Latin American nationals are taking their own capital out. The implication is that investment will not be profitable in Latin America until policies are put in place that will lead to repatriation of capital.

Professor Dornbusch's study examines in detail the main motives and vehicles for the flight of capital from Latin America during the 1980s. It also presents a cogent analysis of the macroeconomic implications of this capital flight, describes its economic cost to the region, and suggests possible remedies.

Although this paper represents the personal views of the author and does not necessarily reflect the opinion of the Inter-American Development Bank, we feel that the analysis it contains greatly enriches the current debate on issues of importance to the countries of the region.

Nohra Rey de Marulanda

Manager
Economic and Social
Development Department

CONTENTS

OVERVIEW

Until the late 1970s, the flight of capital from Latin America had been sporadic and was associated primarily with instability in one particular country or other. The striking fact of the 1980s, however, has been of Latin American capital flight on a scale sufficiently large to make it a key source of macroeconomic instability and debt accumulation throughout the region. Table 1 shows cumulative capital flight from Latin America over the period 1975-1985 somewhat in excess of US$100 billion, or about US$265 per capita (IMF estimate). Even that high number may be an underestimate of the actual *stock* of capital flight. A return of this capital is often advocated as a central part of solving debt problems for both debtor governments and creditors.

Table I. Worldwide Capital Flight (1975-1985)
(Cumulative, billions of U.S. dollars)

Africa	28.5
Asia	18.3
Europe	24.0
Non-Oil Middle East	6.2
Western Hemisphere	106.6

Source: Deppler and Williamson (1987), IMF.

The present study is in six parts.[1] The first section examines motives and vehicles for capital flight and presents the available estimates of its actual extent. The second section gives case studies of Argentina and Mexico. The third section evaluates the macroeconomic implications of capital flight, and the fourth considers possible remedies for the problem. The fifth section considers various aspects of the return of capital following stabilization, and the sixth presents concluding observations.

[1] *I am indebted to Eliana Cardoso, Alejandro Reynoso, and an anonymous referee for helpful suggestions.*

MOTIVES, VEHICLES, AND MEASURES OF CAPITAL FLIGHT

When capital moves from Tokyo to New York, it is called a capital flow or portfolio investment; when it moves from Mexico City or Buenos Aires to Miami, it is called capital flight. Yet both kinds of foreign investment are driven by a profit motive. It is immediately clear that definitional issues will be important in order to identify what precisely is meant by capital flight. Like the proverbial elephant, it is difficult to define but totally obvious when a concrete instance is seen. A good working definition is the one provided by Deppler and Williamson (1987):

> *Capital flight may be defined as the acquisition or retention of a claim on nonresidents that is motivated by the owner's concern that the value of the asset would be subject to discrete losses if the claims continued to be held domestically.*

This definition invites discussion of what kinds of events might bring about these "discrete" losses, thereby constituting motives for capital flight. The definition involving discrete losses is appropriate whenever major realignments of the exchange rate or political shifts are at issue. It is also quite possible to envisage a situation of what might be called low-level capital flight—a steady capital outflow motivated by tax fraud or simply a concern to diversify asset holdings in a way that is impossible in the domestic capital market. Even though the latter form of capital flight does not occur in waves, the cumulative loss of resources in an economy is naturally of consequence. If savings are invested outside the country, they are not at hand to support domestic growth.

Motives

In this section, we review the following four predominant motives for capital flight: expected major changes in the exchange rate, political risk, financial repression, and tax considerations.

Expected Devaluation

The leading motive for capital flight is a desire to exploit the opportunity for exchange gains. When exchange rates are ostensibly overvalued, it becomes increasingly clear that a major devaluation lies ahead. An asset holder who shifts out of peso assets into dollar assets can in time be assured of a capital gain. The larger the expected depreciation, the larger is the capital gain that can be anticipated. With a 30 percent nominal depreciation over three months, for example, a well-timed round trip would yield an annual rate of return of 186 percent. This return will often be large relative to the interest rate that can be earned on domestic assets. As a result, asset holders will shift from domestic assets to assets located abroad.

The leading reason that an overvaluation of the exchange rate might build up is a policy that seeks to stabilize inflationary pressures by slowing down the rate of depreciation, thereby gradually building up an unsustainable real appreciation (as discussed later in more detail). Instances also exist of external shocks that make a given real exchange rate unsustainable. A country's terms of trade might worsen, for instance, or an inability to roll over debt and pay interest out of new money might arise. One way or another, the market recognizes that the exchange rate cannot last, and hence assets shift abroad to take advantage of the likely capital gains. We later consider as a case study the Mexican experience of 1982, which is a textbook example of an episode of overvaluation. The country's 1988 experience may turn out to be yet another textbook example; every time the real exchange rate appreciates significantly, there occurs a massive outflow of capital.

Politics

The second reason for capital flight is politics. Changes of regime lead to capital flight, particularly when an abrupt shift in economic orientation toward the left is involved. The reason is that asset holders fear levies, taxation, or expropriation. To forestall losses, they move at least part of their assets out of reach of the suspect government.

Such politically motivated capital flight is a problem not only for developing countries.[2] French history, in fact, is replete with it. Prior to the Poincaré stabilization in 1926, massive capital flight took place out of asset holders' fear of a wealth tax. And again in 1980 and 1988, capital flight from France was significant. In Latin America, massive capital flight is associated with the advent of populist governments or with the turn of governments toward populism. Mexico under López Portillo, García's Peru, Argentina under the Peronists, and Allende's Chile are examples. But capital flight can begin even before the populist government arrives. A case in point is the significant capital flight from Brazil that started in 1986-1987, anticipating a shift toward the left in the country's politics.

Politically motivated capital flight may be separate in principle from that motivated by exchange rate considerations, but in fact the two tend to come together. Populist governments will tend to overvalue exchange rates, for example, and thus often more than one reason exists to shift assets abroad.

Financial Repression and Missing Markets

Reynoso (1988a,b) has introduced an important extra dimension in interpreting capital flight. He observes that the flight of capital from Mexico in 1982 was the result of the absence of financial markets in that country. The regulation of

---

[2] *See Brown (1987) for a history of flight of capital from developed countries.*

deposit rates and the absence of a money market (with Treasury bills, CDs, and secondary trading) implied that the return differential between New York (including steady depreciation) and Mexico was simply too large for asset holders and institutions not to move assets abroad.

The introduction of a money market in Mexico in 1986-1987 mitigated this problem. Now there are Mexican claims that yield an interest rate in excess of the New York rate adjusted for depreciation. As a result, the previous disintermediation has disappeared. Specifically, following the 1982 experience of massive capital flight, the Mexican government moved from a fixed discount rate for Treasury bills to an auction mechanism. Although negative real interest rates do arise on occasion, the pattern of persistent and large negative returns no longer exists. As a result, capital flight has become less of an issue—even when inflation increases sharply, as in 1987. The liberalization of domestic financial markets went farther in 1986-1987, when private indexed and nonindexed flexible-rate debt instruments were allowed.

Tax Considerations

Asset holders are concerned with maximizing their after-tax income and wealth. This is always possible when foreign tax rates are lower than those in the country of residence. In a few situations it may be legal not to declare and pay taxes on assets located abroad, as is apparently the case with Argentina (for reasons that are hard to understand). Most often, however, outright tax fraud is involved—aided and abetted, of course, by industrialized countries that offer tax-free investment opportunities for nonresidents. The attraction of tax fraud increases in proportion to the differential between the marginal tax rate in the home country and the zero tax rate in the host location. Thus, if the home country levies an exceptionally high marginal tax rate on particular income groups, it is not surprising that these groups place assets abroad.

Having identified the various motives for capital flight, we now turn to the vehicles. In our later discussion on policy, we shall return to the motives for capital flight, in assessing remedies. Meanwhile, the modeling of the capital flight motive is discussed in Appendix A.

Vehicles

How do residents of a developing country acquire external assets?[3] There are three principal channels: purchase of foreign currency, authorized capital transfers, and misinvoicing. The first and most obvious way, the purchase of actual U.S. currency in the open or black market, is the "retail level" approach to capital flight. It is, in toto, quantitatively important; although no precise estimates exist, it is believed, for example, that several billion dollars of U.S. currency are held in Argentina. To the extent that U.S. currency serves as both

[3] *See, in particular, Walter (1985) on the vehicles and outlets of capital flight. See, too, Dornbusch (1987).*

a medium of exchange and a store of value, this number is not surprising. A holding of only US$50 per capita with a population of 30 million already comes to US$1.5 billion! The only reason these holdings can be at all significant is that dollarization is so widespread.

"Wholesale" capital flight takes place via either of the remaining two channels—legal capital outflows (openly financed by the central bank) or misinvoicing of trade flows. The simplest case of legal capital outflows obtains in those instances in which the central bank allows transfers abroad at the official exchange rate. Because capital controls are cumbersome and, in some countries, very ineffective, many governments do in fact in one form or another authorize transfers at the official exchange rate. In those instances there can of course be massive capital flight in response to a ripe overvaluation. Mexico is a case in point; for most of the past decade, there were no capital controls in place because the government felt that controls could not be made effective, and as a result, capital transfers could take place in the open market.

When capital cannot legally be transferred or when underground earnings and assets are involved, misinvoicing of trade transactions may occur. Overinvoicing of imports and underinvoicing of exports permit economic agents to acquire foreign exchange for their own account or to sell to third parties in the black market. In industrialized and developing countries alike, "leads and lags" peak in periods preceding devaluation; in developing countries, misinvoicing also increases significantly at such times. (Interestingly, on the import side, the misinvoicing of trade transactions is subject to conflicting temptations; the tendency to overinvoice imports to effect capital flight is tempered by the desire to underinvoice imports to avoid import taxes. Which of the two effects dominates depends on the relative size of the import duty and the black-market premium. On the export side, underinvoicing serves both capital flight and duty evasion, and any export subsidies lost are probably small anyway because of GATT rules; as a result, export underinvoicing tends to be rampant.) Estimates of export underinvoicing can be obtained from a comparison of the relevant import values of all countries with the export value of a particular exporting country. Using these trade data, Cuddington (1986) reports that in the period 1977-1983, average underinvoicing of exports in Argentina was 19.6 percent; Brazil, 12.7 percent; Chile, 12.8 percent; Mexico, 33.6 percent; and Uruguay, 27.8 percent.

Once assets have been placed abroad, whether through legal foreign exchange market transactions or by misinvoicing of trade flows, asset holders must choose in what form to hold them.[4] The only statistics available about how external assets are held pertain to bank deposits by nonbank depositors. Table 2 shows these data for several countries.

Brazil apparently did not suffer much capital flight until 1987. This contrasts sharply with Venezuela, Mexico, and Argentina, where the currency experiments of the 1980s led to massive capital flight. Because Table 2 shows only bank deposits, however, it does exclude holdings of financial assets (Treasury bills,

---

[4] *See Walter (1985) and Henry (1986) on where the money goes.*

Table 2. Latin America: Cross-Border Bank Deposits (1981 and 1987)

By Nationals of:	1981	1989	1987 Per Capita Deposits (dollars per capita)
	(billions of U.S. dollars)		
Argentina	6.4	7.7	241
Brazil	3.5	12.8	88
Mexico	9.4	19.5	235
Peru	0.6	2.5	114
Venezuela	15.6	13.8	726
Philippines	0.5	1.0	17
Egypt	1.6	4.0	92
Korea	0.3	0.6	14

Source: IMF, International Financial Statistics.

CDs, and stocks), direct investment by fully owned corporations (the Brazilian Globo television chain buying U.S. television stations), and holdings of real estate. The deposit numbers are thus only part of the entire stock of external assets.

Measures of Capital Flight[5]

Disagreement exists as to an operational definition of capital flight, and specifically as to whether capital flight is to be defined in terms of its consequences or its motivations.

Cuddington (1986) and Cumby and Levich (1987) argue for a welfare-theoretic basis of definition. For them the distinguishing characteristic of capital flight, as opposed to other capital flows, is that its *consequence* is national disutility. They argue therefore that capital flight could be defined as a capital outflow regarded as disadvantageous by the national authorities. Taking this position to its logical end, all private capital outflows from developing countries, be they short term or long term, be they portfolio or equity investment, could be termed capital flight. Because developing countries are generally capital poor and because all capital outflows reduce the resources available to these countries for the development process, thus representing a loss of potential growth, all capital outflows could be termed capital flight from the point of view of consequences.

This concept gives rise to a broad measure of capital flight defined as the identified acquisitions of external assets (except official reserves), plus recorded errors and omissions in the balance of payments. Errors and omissions are thus implicitly considered in their entirety as capital transactions that can be regarded

[5] *This section draws on Cardoso and Dornbusch (1988).*

as capital flight. This definition corresponds to those used by the World Bank (1985), Erbe (1985), and Rodríguez (1986), for example. It is measured as a residual—gross capital inflows, less the current account deficit, less the acquisition of official reserves.[6] Estimates for capital flight based on this definition are presented later in Table 3, under the heading "broad measure."

Several authors, among them Dooley (1986), Lessard and Williamson (1987), and Deppler and Williamson (1987), argue that capital flight should be distinguished by its *motivations*, not by its consequences for national welfare. No doubt a definition based on investors' motives for acquiring claims on nonresidents involves a good amount of judgment in order to distinguish "fleeing" capital from capital flows that occur in the course of portfolio diversification. According to these authors, although all capital flows are motivated by endeavors to maximize return on capital, the specific motivation for capital flight is fear of capital loss from risks of expropriation, debt repudiation, or the introduction of new market distortions such as capital controls, taxation, or financial repression. To be classified as capital flight, the capital outflow must be a response to losses or risks perceived to be large in relation to the moving capital. It is not easy, however, to make operational use of this concept.

Dooley (1986) and Khan and Ul Haque (1987) propose to measure capital flight as that part of a country's stock of foreign assets that does not yield a recorded inflow of investment income credits. The presumption is that only the retention of income abroad is indicative of capital flight. Capital flight is computed as the difference between total foreign assets and the stock of nonflight capital. This method first estimates gross capital outflows by subtracting the current account deficit less the part financed by non-debt-creating flows (direct investment flows, changes in international reserves held by the central bank, and changes in net foreign assets of domestic banks) from changes in external debt. The resulting gross capital outflows reflect the total stock of external claims of the country over a period of time. As a second step, nonflight capital is estimated as the capitalized value of recorded investment income credits, using an appropriate interest rate. The difference between this value of nonflight capital and the estimated total stock of external claims is considered to be capital flight. In Table 3, this measure is called "derived measure."

[6] *The capital flight definition adopted by Morgan Guaranty (1986) also measures capital flight as a residual. In addition to the current account deficit and the increase in official reserves, Morgan's definition subtracts the increase in short-term foreign assets of the banking system from total capital inflows.*

Table 3. Capital Flight from Capital-Importing Developing Countries* (1975-1985)
(Billions of U.S. dollars)

	1975-78	1979-82	1983-85	Increase from End-1974 to End-1985 in Stocks Outstanding
Broad Measure	15.3	30.0	17.9	235
Derived Measure	5.6	26.4	12.5	165

** Country classification from IMF,* World Economic Outlook.
Source: Deppler and Williamson (1987), Table 1.

Two other measures commonly used are the private claims measure (Conesa 1986) and the "hot money" measure (Cuddington 1986). Cuddington adds net short-term capital outflows of the nonbank private sector to recorded errors and omissions to obtain a measure that views capital flight as similar to flows of hot money, that is, funds that respond quickly to changes in expected returns or to changes in risk.

The conceptual differences among the various measures will naturally lead to different estimates of capital flight. Even though some measures are conceptually broader than others, data problems can be large enough to offset differences in coverage and produce unexpected ordering of estimates.[7]

In Appendix B, we show detailed estimates (updating Cumby and Levich 1987) for several Latin American countries, using alternative definitions. In Table 4, we report only the World Bank measure for two subperiods.

Table 4. Latin America: Estimates of Capital Flight (1979-1987)
(Cumulative, billions of U.S. dollars)

	Argentina	Brazil	Mexico	Peru	Venezuela
1979-82	22.4	5.8	25.3	n.a.	20.7
1983-87	6.8	24.8	35.3	3.3	18.9

Source: Cumby and Levich (1987) and update by the author.

[7] *Deppler and Williamson (1987) offer a detailed discussion of data problems.*

As the discussion makes clear, measurement of the stock of capital flight is exceptionally difficult even at the conceptual level. The situation is exacerbated by the quality of actual data. The flows are uncertain because of such issues as underinvoicing of trade, undisclosed military imports, and the classification of external asset transactions by banks and state enterprises. The stock position is uncertain because there are no detailed statistics (except, to some extent, for bank deposits) on foreign asset holdings by residents of debtor countries. Changes in these stocks over time depend, as noted by Cuddington (1987), on flows, on capital gains, and on interest earnings. Because much of the capital flight occurred in the late 1970s, the accumulated interest over the past ten years, assuming a 10 percent rate of return in dollars, would make each dollar that left in the late 1970s equal to 2.5 dollars in the late 1980s.

COUNTRY EXPERIENCE WITH CAPITAL FLIGHT

Two kinds of evidence bear on the determinants of capital flight: econometric regression analysis and case studies. We look first at econometric evidence and then consider some episodes from the capital flight histories of Argentina and Mexico.

Econometric Evidence

Econometric work on capital flight has been done by Cuddington (1986, 1987) and Dooley (1986). In this work, capital flight is explained by the rate of return. In a seven-country study, Dooley finds that inflation differentials, depreciation-adjusted interest differentials, and country risk premiums explain well the extent of capital flight. Specifically, the higher a country's inflation relative to that of the United States and the lower its depreciation-adjusted interest rate, the higher is capital flight. The coefficients, as seen in the following Dooley equation, are highly significant:

$$\begin{aligned} K &= \underset{(4.22)}{20.5\,\mathrm{INF}} + \underset{(3.27)}{13.1\,\mathrm{DIFF}} - \underset{(-2.56)}{1.23\,\mathrm{RP}} \\ R^2 &= 0.77 \end{aligned}$$

where K is capital flight,
INF is the inflation differential,
DIFF is the depreciation-adjusted interest differential, and
RP is a country's external risk premium.

The Dooley model envisages capital flight as a response to differential risk of residents and nonresidents. Nonresidents lending to the country (perhaps with dollar-denominated debt) are protected against taxation or inflationary erosion of their assets in a way that residents are not. Thus, capital flight is part of an intermediation via the world capital market providing residents with safer assets. This intermediation requires that nonresidents perceive little risk involved in holding a country's external assets so that nonresidents are willing to lend when residents are not. Accordingly, if the external risk premium (that is, default risk) increases, the asymmetry between residents and nonresidents declines; as a result, there is less scope for capital flight. This explains the significant negative coefficient on the measure of the external risk premium in the Dooley equation.

Case Studies

The following case studies of capital flight in Argentina and Mexico illustrate very well the way in which large expected return differentials between home and foreign assets bring about massive capital flight.

Argentina

The Argentine government, under Finance Minister Martínez de Hoz, experimented in 1978-1981 with an inflation stabilization program based on the exchange rate. This *tablita* mechanism of a gradual, pre-announced phasing down of exchange depreciation led eventually to a massive overvaluation of the real exchange rate and, as a consequence, to enormous capital flight. In the initial stages, the story was complicated by a financial reform that opened up the domestic capital market and international capital flows.

Before examining this process in some detail, let us get an overview of the 1977-1982 period in Argentina. Table 5 shows the country's balance of payments statistics for that entire period. Following financial reform and given high average real interest rates at home, firms borrowed abroad in preference to borrowing in the home market. In this period, the increase in the gross external debt had a counterpart in capital imports by firms and reserve gains by the central bank, particularly in 1979. Financial reform was not the only reason for the early capital inflows; the *tablita* certainly was part of the attraction.

Table 5. Argentina: Balance of Payments and Gross External Debt (1977-1982)
(Billions of U.S. dollars)

	1977	1978	1979	1980	1981	1982
Current Account	1.3	1.8	-0.5	-4.7	-4.7	-2.4
Non-Interest	1.8	2.6	0.6	-2.6	-0.9	2.6
Capital Inflows	1.3	1.3	4.7	2.6	1.5	-2.3
Firms	1.1	0.7	4.2	2.0	-1.1	-3.1
Banks	0.2	0.1	-0.0	-0.4	0.0	1.1
Government	-0.0	0.5	0.5	0.9	2.5	-0.4
Balance of Payments	2.5	3.2	4.4	-2.5	-3.4	-5.1
Gross External Debt	9.7	12.5	19.0	27.2	35.7	43.6

Source: Indicadores de Coyuntura, *various issues.*

The Tablita: The disappointing progress on disinflation had led the government to announce, in December 1978, the *tablita* disinflation strategy based on reduced, pre-announced rates of devaluation. The theory behind this disinflation policy relied on the Chicago School "law of one price" popularized for traded goods by Harry Johnson and Robert Mundell. This view held that prices in any country were strongly linked to their world price and that, given this link, a policy of depreciation inevitably meant inflation, thereby requiring further depreciation—which would in turn lead to more inflation.

In order to break this vicious cycle of inflation and depreciation, Argentine policymakers opted to set a path of decelerating exchange depreciation, hoping that it would feed through into reduced inflation. At the same time, targets for public sector wages and prices, as well as for the expansion of domestic credit, were set. The Plan of December 20th had the following specific announcements:[8]

- Public sector wages and prices were to rise at a monthly rate of 4 percent over the subsequent eight months.
- Domestic credit was to grow at 4 percent per month during the first semester of 1979.
- Exchange depreciation was to be 5.4 percent for January 1979 and decline from that level by 0.2 percent per month until August 1981.

Three linkages from depreciation to inflation were expected. First, expectations of depreciation were built into pricing; reducing the rate of depreciation would lead firms to reduce their inflation forecasts and hence their price increases. Second, the rate of increase of import prices would be dampened automatically by reduced depreciation. Third, firms competing with importables would be forced into price discipline. Reduced depreciation was thus thought to operate through various channels in reducing inflation.

Particular emphasis was placed on the expectations channel. To reinforce this effect, the future path of the exchange rate was pre-announced. Thus, in December 1978 the authorities announced depreciation rates falling from 5.2 to 4 percent per month over the next eight months. This process was followed until 1981, when the system broke down as a result of the progressive overvaluation shown in Figure 1.

The law of one price was also expected to apply to interest rates. Hence it was thought that pre-fixing of the rate of depreciation would rapidly reduce domestic interest rates to those prevailing abroad, adjusted, of course, for the rate of depreciation. With an interest rate (including spread) in New York of 1.5215 percent per month, for example, and a depreciation rate of 4 percent per month, the Argentine interest rate should be 5.59 percent per month.

Table 6 shows Argentina's quarterly rates of depreciation, the CPI inflation rate, the nominal interest rate, and the real exchange rate.

If announcements are believed, the difference between nominal interest rates and the rate of depreciation directs the choice between borrowing in Argentina and borrowing abroad. When the Argentine interest rate exceeds the announced rate of depreciation, there should be borrowing in the world market.

---

[8] *See Dornbusch (1985), Fernández (1985), and Rodríguez (1982).*

Figure 1. Argentina: The Real Exchange Rate (1977-1981)
(Index: 1980-82=100)

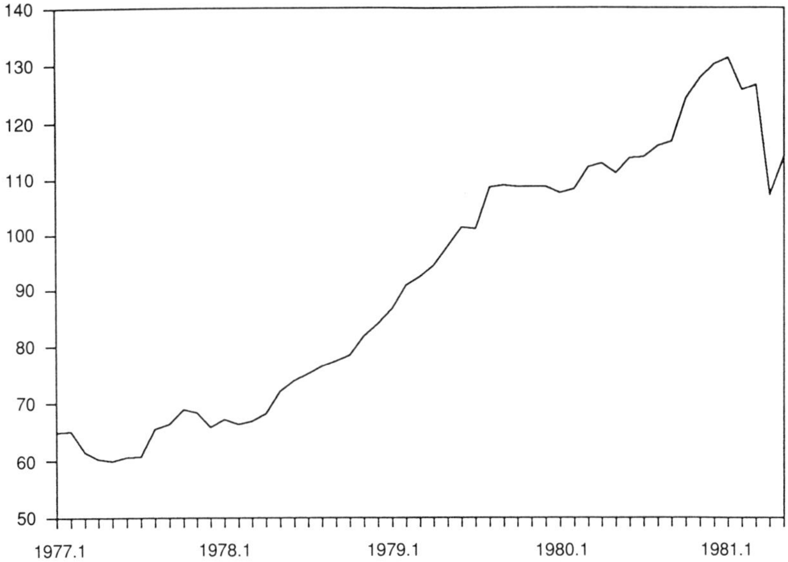

Table 6. Argentina: Indicators of the Tablita Period (1978-1981)

(Quarterly percentage rates, except as noted)

			Interest		Real Exchange Rate	
	Depreciation	Inflation	Pas.	Act.	Morgan	PD/PM
1978						
I	21.4	28.1	27.7	37.8	82	71
II	11.5	26.3	22.3	26.9	87	80
III	8.3	19.4	20.7	25.0	93	89
IV	15.5	27.8	21.5	24.6	100	100
1979						
I	15.5	31.5	20.7	23.3	110	109
II	14.2	27.0	20.9	23.0	120	109
III	12.2	27.3	23.2	25.7	130	117
IV	10.2	11.0	20.6	23.5	133	115
1980						
I	8.3	14.2	16.6	19.4	134	110
II	6.5	15.5	15.0	18.1	137	114
III	4.5	9.7	16.2	19.9	141	116
IV	3.1	14.2	15.1	18.8	156	114
1981						
I	17.6	14.0	21.7	26.7	157	107

Note: Interest rates refer to active and passive rates. Inflation rate refers to nonagricultural wholesale prices. The real exchange rate is an index with base 1978: IV = 100. The Morgan Guaranty measure compares nonfood wholesale prices in Argentina to a trade-weighted average abroad. The second measure of the real exchange rate refers to the relative wholesale price of domestic goods and imports, PD/PM.

Source: Fernández (1985) and Morgan Guaranty.

The year 1979 is a typical year for the combination of policies to attract capital inflows. Interest rates are very high relative to the rate of depreciation. The return from borrowing in New York and lending in Buenos Aires in December 1979, for example, is above 50 percent per year! Moreover, because of high (and growing) reserves, the policy is believable. The moderate current account deficit supports the idea that the exchange rate policy is sustainable. As a result, capital inflows are exceptionally high throughout the year. The increase in external debt exceeds the capital flow, but not by a wide margin. In 1980, real interest rates turn sharply positive, which suggests that financial market integration is as imperfect as goods market integration, because the government could implement a tight domestic money strategy even under a pre-fixed exchange rate regime.

The Collapse: The large discrepancy between depreciation and inflation resulted in a gradual appreciation of the real exchange rate. Between March 1976 and December 1978, the real exchange rate (as shown in Figure 1) had already appreciated by 20 percent. During the first year of the *tablita*, real appreciation amounted to 33 percent and was a further 17 percent in 1980. Only in 1980 did it become widely apparent that the disinflation strategy might fail. Inflation had declined, but not by an amount sufficient to justify a belief that exchange rate-based disinflation could be pursued long enough to reduce inflation to tolerable levels.

The increasingly apparent overvaluation was not the only reason for unrest. The failure of major banks, resulting from dishonesty in management, had created financial uncertainty, forcing the government to take them over. Because of very high real interest rates, which persisted for an extended period, the government also had started accumulating internal debts. This combination of factors brought about a wave of capital outflows. Beginning in the second quarter of 1980, the Central Bank of Argentina experienced reserve losses. For the year, reserve losses came to nearly US$3 billion, as shown in Figure 2. In the first quarter of 1981, reserve losses were US$3 billion.

The current account deteriorated seriously beginning in 1980. The main reason for the worsening was a large increase in imports; the huge real appreciation, along with some trade liberalization, had led to an increase in imports of nearly US$4 billion. Interest payments increased, but the increase in exports more than compensated. Moving into 1981, the increase in world interest rates started to show up massively in the current account.

These actual and prospective reserve losses reinforced the belief that the exchange rate policy could not be sustained and thus led to even more capital flight. Another important factor was the change from one president to another. In October 1980, the presidency of Viola was announced; from that time on, Martínez de Hoz was a lame duck economics minister. The new president was unwilling to commit himself ahead of time to a Martínez de Hoz-style policy. As a result, overt ambiguity existed concerning policy continuity. The public drew the obvious conclusion and shifted into foreign assets. The large amount of capital flight, offset only incompletely by public sector borrowing in world

Figure 2. Argentina: International Reserves (1978-1982)
(Billions of dollars)

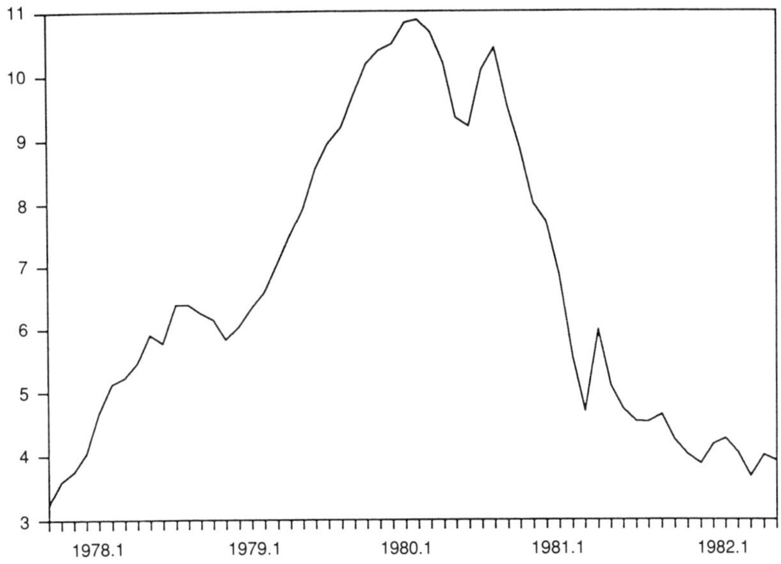

markets, implied unsustainable reserve losses. By late 1980, the exchange rate announcements ceased to be believed; in February 1981, Martínez de Hoz was forced to violate the precommitted exchange rate targets by a 10 percent devaluation on top of the 2 percent pre-announced depreciation.

Mexico

Figure 3 shows the Mexican real exchange rate (1970-1988) as reported by Morgan Guaranty. This measure is calculated as nonfood manufacturing wholesale prices in Mexico relative to the prices in a common currency of its trading partners. Both 1976 and 1981-1982 were periods of dollarization and massive capital flight. The general phenomenon of flight from the peso has given rise to an entire literature on "peso problems" and on "speculative attacks" on unsustainable exchange rate regimes.[9]

[9] *See Lizondo (1983), Krugman (1979), Flood and Garber (1984), and Blanco and Garber (1986).*

Mexico in 1982: In August 1982, Mexico declared a moratorium on debt payments. The sources of the Mexican debt crisis of 1982 have been reported in a number of studies.[10] What were the factors chiefly responsible for the crisis?

- Last year of the sexenio. Election year in Mexico traditionally is an occasion for macroeconomic recklessness, just as 1976 had been.
- A vastly expansionary fiscal policy. In only three years, the primary budget deficit increased from 3 percent to 8 percent of GDP. This deterioration occurred despite a major increase in the real price of oil, which directly benefited the budget on the receipts side. As Zedillo (1985, p. 310) notes, "To the international bankers' comfort, Mexico became the 'champion of absorption'... not only of its own oil revenue but of that of others as well."
- A substantially overvalued real exchange rate. Between 1979 and 1981, the real exchange rate appreciated by almost 25 percent.
- Persistently negative real interest rates. In 1982, real interest rates averaged -20 percent on one-month deposits, as shown in Figure 4. Adjusting for exchange depreciation, the losses on domestic assets were even larger. The negative interest rates on domestic deposits combined with the overvaluation to create a massive incentive for dollarization and flight of capital abroad.[11] Capital flight reached at least US$17 billion in 1981-1982.

Solís and Zedillo (1985) have analyzed the increase in debt in the period 1979-1981. They conclude that most of the increase was the result of domestic policy shocks; capital flight is plainly the most significant factor. Their results are summarized in Table 7.

Table 7. Mexico's Sources of Increase in the External Debt (1979-1981)
(Percentage of total debt increase)

	1979	1980	1981
External Shocks	33.1	28.7	16.2
Interest Rate	25.9	27.2	17.8
Internal Shocks	66.9	71.3	83.8
Capital Flight	49.7	44.3	55.7

Source: Solís and Zedillo (1985, Table 10-6).

[10] *For extensive references, see Dornbusch (1988).*

[11] *Dollarization refers to the holding of dollar-denominated deposits in Mexican banks, the so-called Mexdollars. The term also more broadly denotes the flight from local currency to dollars to be held either in the form of U.S. currency or deposits in U.S. banks. The size of Mexican deposits in the United States is demonstrated by the fact that more than 20 percent of deposits in the El Paso (Texas) banks belong to Mexicans. On dollarization, see especially Ortiz (1983), Ramírez-Rojas (1985), and Reynoso (1988b).*

Figure 3. Mexico: Real Exchange Rate (1970-1988)
(Index: 1980-82=100)

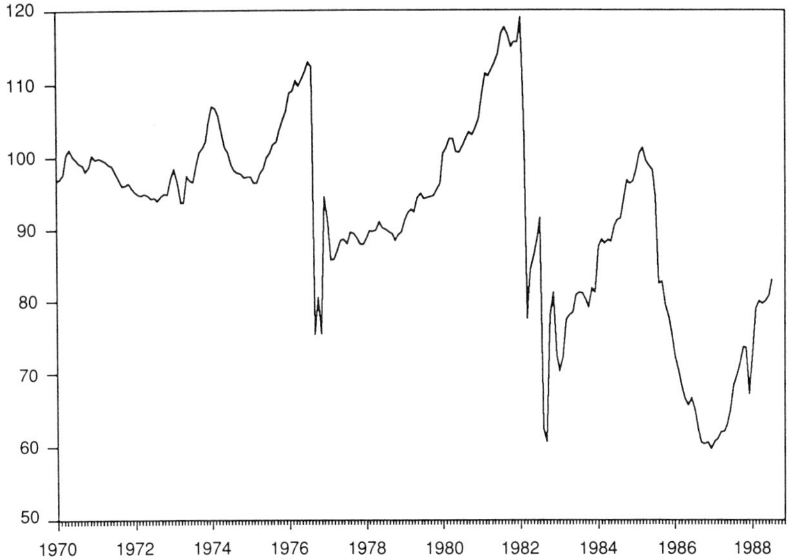

Figure 4. Mexico: Real Deposit Yield (1977-1988)
(Percent per year, three-month moving average)

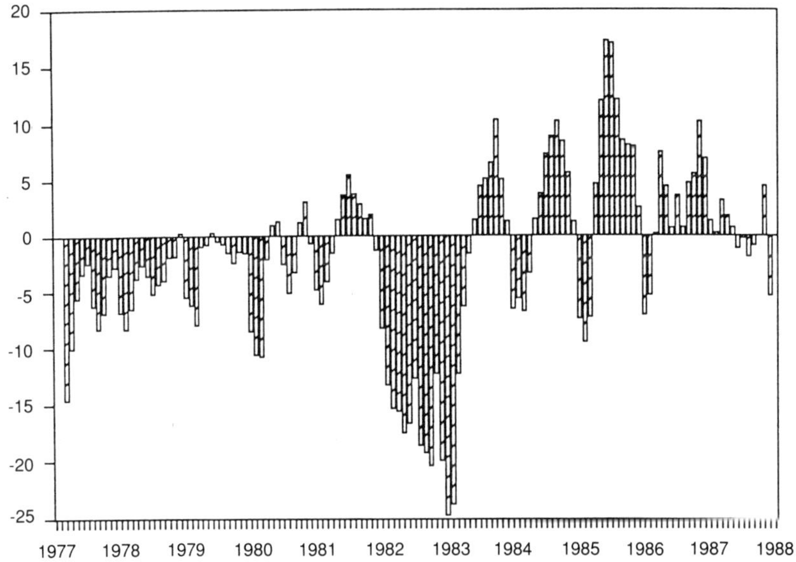

The attribution of two-thirds or more of the debt increase to "internal shocks" leaves no doubt that the 1982 crisis was "made in Mexico." By contrast, much of the adjustment difficulty of the period after 1982 resulted from a very unfavorable external environment and the intensive vulnerability imposed by a large debt.[12]

Mexico in 1988: The issue of capital flight arose again in 1988. In a program of inflation stabilization, the government reached agreements with the unions and some firms to stop wage and price increases. As a counterpart, there was a freeze on public sector prices and, importantly, on the exchange rate. The program went into effect early in 1988. But because some private prices were outside the agreement and did not stop rising, the program led to the gradual real appreciation of the peso, as shown in Figure 3.

At the outset the appreciation did not raise questions because there was a sufficiently large cushion of competitiveness. But a 1.2 percent real appreciation per month must ultimately raise questions. The question is then how to shift from a nominal exchange rate freeze to one of a stable real exchange rate. If the nominal fixed exchange rate is continued too long, as in Argentina, there is an expectation of a corrective maxi-devaluation. As a result, capital flight will develop, which in turn *forces* the maxi-devaluation. Thus, there is a self-fulfilling character to this process.

The way to avoid a collapse of the stabilization program is to move smoothly from the freeze to a crawling peg regime, *without* a maxi-devaluation. This presupposes that the transition is achieved in time, so that the real exchange rate is sustainable once the move to a crawling peg is made. Mexico in fact made that move at the beginning of 1989, thus avoiding an exchange crisis.

---

[12] *See Dornbusch (1988) for a detailed discussion of the Mexican experience.*

MACROECONOMIC IMPLICATIONS OF CAPITAL FLIGHT

The costs of capital flight are of three broad types.[13] First, capital flight tends to destabilize macroeconomic management. This assertion is very familiar from the discussion of the interwar period; Nurkse (1946) argued that capital flight from France destabilized the exchange rate and hence the budget and macroeconomic management. (Opponents of that view claimed that poor policy itself, not speculation, was the cause of instability. This is often correct also, but there is an important qualification. Policies are not, in fact, exogenous. A government not subject to the threat of capital flight may be able to pursue certain policies that become impossible with capital flight. Thus, if there are multiple equilibria, it is clearly possible that capital flight can constitute at least one active source of macroeconomic difficulties.) With capital flight possibilities, real exchange rates have to be invariably on the defensive side, and interest rates need to be sufficiently high to reward asset holders for the "risk" of holding domestic assets. The political consequence is that the middle and upper classes are having their assets protected at the expense of wage earners. (Of course, to assert that capital flight destabilizes macroeconomic management does beg the question of what is the counterfactual experiment. If macroeconomic policies *were* "credible," or if an effective control of capital flows *could* be implemented, then such a system would naturally be preferred over one in which high real interest rates and a low real wage are required to create the confidence needed to keep asset holders from shifting into foreign securities.) Capital flight additionally implies that residents of a country will tend to hold less domestic currency and more foreign currency and assets; to the extent that seigniorage is used as a means of financing budget deficits, reduced seigniorage implies increased inflation, higher taxes, or reduced spending.

Second, capital flight undermines tax morality. This occurs in several ways. Overinvoicing and underinvoicing of trade are often immediate by-products of moving assets abroad. But underinvoicing of exports invariably filters down into the tax transactions of exporting firms and is also reflected in reduced tax payments. Once assets are abroad, it would be altogether exceptional if taxes were paid on the earnings. Hence tax revenue is also reduced at this level. Once external assets have become part of the culture, they become convenient vehicles for the payment of bribes and for fraudulent dealings.

Third, the cost of capital flight can also be stated in terms of growth. When a certain percentage of GNP is transferred abroad year after year, fewer resources are available for domestic investment. External holdings of assets are important

[13] *See Cuddington (1986) for a discussion of these issues.*

in a development context, because they represent savings not available for *domestic* capital formation. But the capital flight is also of interest in the context of the debt crisis. Rather than financing imports of capital goods, for example, export earnings finance (via underinvoicing) the building up of external asset positions. The reduced capital formation implies slower growth and, hence, a less rapid rate of increase in the standard of living of the immobile factor. The same is true when capital flight is financed at the official exchange rate. Whichever the channel through which capital goes abroad, the resources to finance capital flight become available only through decreasing the country's current account surplus or foreign reserves or through external borrowing. Therefore, fewer resources are ultimately available for domestic capital formation, and the welfare of labor is reduced. When massive episodes of capital flight occur, in the style of Argentina or Mexico, not only does investment fall but also the standard of living of workers is cut dramatically to provide financing for the capital escape.

POLICY OPTIONS AND PROBLEMS

The best possible approach to solving the capital flight problem is to avoid the underlying conditions that create capital flight: high inflation, exchange rate overvaluation, and financial instability. In order to do this, the government should avoid yield differentials that are both large and persistent. This implies that large budget deficits cannot be financed by an inflation tax without the risk of accelerating inflation and accelerating capital flight. The higher the inflation rate and the resulting tax on domestic assets, the larger is the incentive to shift assets abroad. The resulting decline in the base of the inflation tax raises the inflation rate required to finance a given deficit, which in turn leads to yet more capital flight and even higher inflation. How far the process goes depends on the extent to which the economy can, in fact, become dollarized. In principle, hyperinflation is a possibility, particularly if the government allows full dollarization of the medium of exchange. The government must recognize that capital flight puts a limit on deficit financing in the sense that it sharply raises the costs of deficit financing and potentially involves *accelerating* inflation.

The government should also avoid one-shot speculative opportunities such as a massive exchange rate overvaluation. A large overvaluation is inevitably followed by corrective depreciation. The larger the overvaluation, the larger is the part of the population that recognizes the capital gain to be obtained from holding external assets and hence the larger is the capital flight. If the capital flight is not fully reversed following depreciation, the permanent social cost of the initial misalignment is yet larger. The only way to avoid these one-shot debacles is a consistent crawling peg exchange rate policy. This avoids having overvaluation arise in the first place and hence keeps a lid on speculative opportunities.

In the real world, however, economic management is often not sufficiently farsighted to avoid instability. Let us suppose, then, that deficits and misalignments of the exchange rate do in fact exist. There are few policy options that would be both effective in stemming capital flight and politically acceptable. The most obvious means is to have high real interest rates and an undervalued exchange rate. High real interest rates will stop investment, however, and an undervalued exchange rate, in addition to the inflationary impact of depreciation, implies a low standard of living for wage earners. Policymakers therefore search for a means to stop capital flight not at the level of fundamentals but rather by attempts to segment asset markets. One possibility is the imposition of capital controls. The other is to try to manage capital flight by domestic dollarization.

Capital Controls

Capital controls have been relatively effective in Korea (and, for some time, in Brazil) but are considered to be almost entirely ineffective in Argentina and Mexico. A large part of the difficulty lies in the geographic conditions of the countries. Mexico, for example, has three thousand miles of border with the United States, and a million Mexicans pass across this border each day. Such conditions make controls of any sort extremely difficult. But part of what determines the effectiveness of capital controls is the government's determination to stop capital flight by effective legal action. It is certainly accepted today that capital controls will not be an answer for many countries.

Brazil is another case in point. Until the early 1980s, capital flight was not a serious issue there, in part because exchange rate overvaluation simply had not been a problem for many years, owing to the fact that the government systematically followed a crawling peg exchange rate regime. This exchange rate policy was complemented in domestic capital markets by a system of indexation that precluded the existence of large negative expected returns. As a consequence, situations of persistent large negative returns on domestic assets never arose, and capital flight was never an issue. After 1983, however, government-created instability in financial markets and in the exchange rate and a perception of deteriorating politics have led to capital flight on a scale that is significant by Brazilian historical standards.

Domestic Dollarization

Mexico, Peru, Uruguay, and other countries have offered domestic, dollar-denominated deposits as a means of avoiding the actual exchange losses associated with capital flight. This would seem to be an excellent policy, in that it offers the public the return it would enjoy in the world market and yet does not cost the country an actual loss of foreign exchange.[14]

The problem of capital flight comes down to the government's attempt to use interest rates and the exchange rate as devices for affecting the distribution of income or wealth. This is the case when the exchange rate is overvalued as a means of raising the standard of living (taxing exporters implicitly) or when deposit rates are kept low so as to extract resources from money holders for the financing of investment or budget deficits. The success of these measures depends critically on the ability to segment markets.

Domestic dollarization does attempt to segment markets but, in doing so, is self-defeating. By giving domestic asset holders the option of holding dollar assets, it in fact creates a vehicle for *domestic* flight from the inflation tax. It thus raises the inflation rate required for the financing of a given deficit. Moreover,

[14] *See Fischer (1982) on the economics of dollarization. Ortiz (1983), Ramírez-Rojas (1985), El-Erian (1988), and Germán Alarco et al. (1985) offer case studies.*

it may raise the inflation rate more than would have been the case without dollar deposits!

To understand the issues, we look at the example of Peru. Figures 5 and 6 show the share of dollar deposits in total quasi-money deposits and the return differential between dollar deposits and deposits denominated in domestic currency. In the period of rising inflation, which went from less than 30 percent in 1976 to more than 100 percent in 1985, the share of dollar deposits increased rapidly.

The actual process of dollarization has two elements. The first is the long-run determinant; the higher the yield differential between dollar-denominated and domestically denominated deposits, the higher the share of dollar deposits. The second is the learning process; following the introduction of dollar deposits, adoption of this new "financial technology" follows a process that has the shape of a logistic curve—a gradual rise at the beginning, then a very steep portion as almost everybody shifts, and then a gradual decline. An econometric estimate, using quarterly data for 1976-1985:Q1, fully supports this theory:[15]

$$\text{DRAT} = \underset{(6.3)}{132.2} - \underset{(-5.2)}{2.4\,\text{RAT}} + \underset{(2.1)}{.34\,\text{DIFF}}$$

$$R2 = 0.42$$

$$DW = 1.91$$

where DRAT is the growth rate of the share of dollar deposits,
RAT is the share of dollar deposits in total deposits, and
DIFF is the yield differential between dollar and national currency deposits.

The equation shows the logistic curve pattern for the adoption of dollar deposits. At the same time, it supports the view that the speed of adjustment and the long-run extent of dollarization depend on the yield differential between dollar-denominated deposits and those denominated in national currency.

Now let us consider this evidence in the context of two national objectives, namely, saving on foreign exchange (by avoiding exchange losses induced by capital flight) and minimizing the inflation rate associated with a given deficit financed by the inflation tax. Domestic dollarization clearly serves the objective of avoiding actual capital outflows. Some need exists for holding dollar reserves as a counterpart to deposits, but that is clearly much less than the one-for-one loss resulting from capital flight.

There is likely to be an offset to this gain, however, in the form of higher inflation. Domestic dollarization facilitates the flight from assets denominated in

[15] *The yield differential data come from Germán Alarco et al. (1985, p. 21), and the deposit data come from the Central Bank of Peru.*

Figure 5. Peru: Dollarization (1976-1985)
(Percentage of total quasi-money)

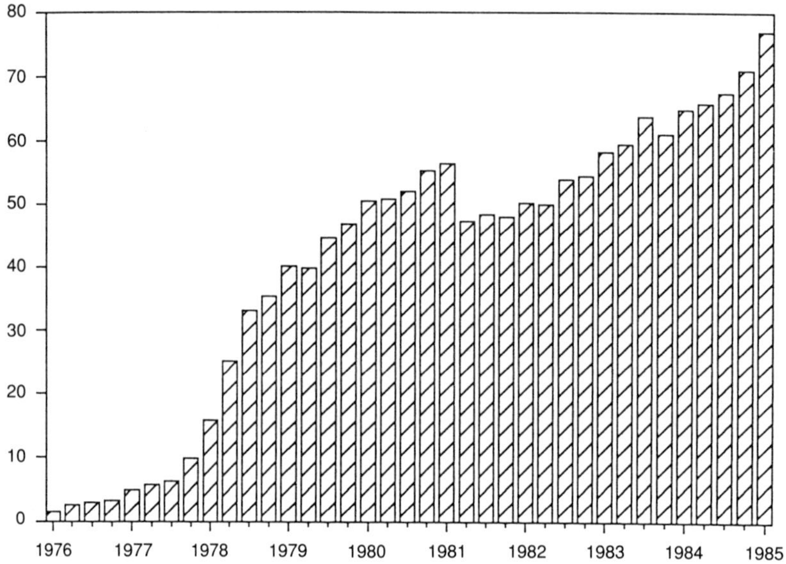

Figure 6: Peru: Return Differential (1976-1985)
(Percent per year)

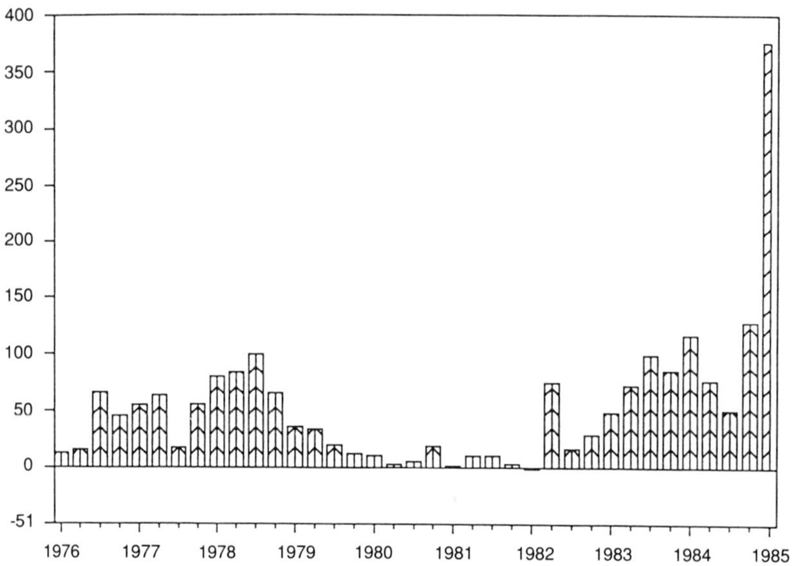

domestic currency. In fact, it puts dollar deposits within easy reach of *anyone*. Normally capital flight requires a certain level of sophistication and balances (except of course for straightforward flight into dollar currency), but domestic dollar deposits can be acquired by a simple banking instruction. As a result, one would expect there to be a larger decline in the demand for domestic balances in the case of domestic dollarization of the banking system than in a situation in which dollars can be held only abroad.

The issue of dollarization then goes squarely to the question of whether a government can successfully segment asset markets. The presence of capital flight itself suggests that limits to this ability do exist. Domestic dollarization is actually a response to a limited ability to segment. It avoids the exchange losses of capital flight, but the price is very likely to be increased inflation.

RETURN OF CAPITAL

A common problem in the aftermath of a stabilization is the lack of a stabilizing capital inflow. Investors have the option of postponing the return of flight capital, and they will wait until the front-loading of returns is sufficient to compensate for the risk of relinquishing liquidity. Investors thus often wait even when interest rates are high and rewarding. Moreover, when capital does return, it chooses a highly liquid form, sitting, so to speak, in the parking lot with the engine running. There is definitely little commitment to a rapid resumption of real investment. The reason for this is residual uncertainty as to whether or not stabilization can, in fact, be sustained. This topic has been addressed in a number of ways in the literature, mostly in terms of irreversible investment decisions. We concentrate here on a very simple, two-period example to make the basic point.

Suppose that investors have a choice between investing in the United States or investing in Mexico. The certain return in the United States in both periods is $R^* = (1+r^*)$. In Mexico, the *certain* first period return is $RM = R^*+m$. In the second period, with probability p events are good and the return is R^G; with probability (1-p) events are bad and the return is only R^B. For simplicity, we assume that the expected return in the second period is equal to the U.S. return, that is $R^* = pR^G + (1-p)R^B$. We assume that investors have the choice of postponing the decision to invest until the uncertainty is resolved. They cannot, however, disinvest in Mexico after the first period if a bad domestic state has materialized. Table 8 shows the alternative returns for the strategy of investing now and for the wait-and-see strategy.

The question now is how large a first-period premium is required to induce investors to accept the uncertainty and invest immediately for two periods. The decision is to invest now or to wait. The relevant criterion for immediate investment is

$$(R^*+m)\,[pR^G + (1-p)\,R^B] \geq R^*\,[pR^G + (1-p)R^*],$$

which, noting that $R^* = pR^G + (1-p)R^B$, reduces to

$$m \geq (1-p)(R^* - R^B).$$

To make an investment, risk-neutral investors thus require a Mexican premium that matches the differences in second-period expected returns on alternative investment opportunities. The reason is that with waiting, an even higher return can be achieved once uncertainty is resolved (or narrowed down). The premium required for immediate investment is higher the larger the probability of a bad domestic state and the larger the discrepancy between the foreign rate of return and that prevailing in an adverse domestic state.

But how can governments reassure investors? The common answer is to bring

Table 8. Mexico: Expected Investment Returns for Alternative Strategies

	Ist Period	2nd Period
Invest in Mexico Now Irreversibly	$R^* + m$	$pR^G + (1\text{-}p)R^B$
Wait-and-See	R^*	$pR^G + (1\text{-}p)R^*$

about a "credible" stabilization, whatever that may mean. In practice, it comes down to high interest rates and an exchange rate so competitive that expected further depreciation is unlikely. High interest rates are counterproductive from the point of view of growth, however, and a low real exchange rate cuts the standard of living and thus reduces demand and profitability for all investments except in the traded goods sector.

If real depreciation is not sufficient, the government is in a very awkward position. Income is being redistributed from labor to capital, but because the real depreciation is not sufficient (in terms of the last equation shown above), the increased profits are taken out as capital flight. Labor will obviously insist that the policy be reversed. This uncertainty as to sustainability is an important feature in understanding the real exchange rate, capital flight relationships, and post-stabilization difficulties in developing countries.

A solution for countries like Mexico or Brazil would be to recycle interest payments—that is, creditors would be paid, but they could not take their interest earnings out of the debtor countries.[16] Creditors would effectively be required to invest these earnings in real assets, loans, or government debt, as they choose. To the extent that debt is serviced in dollars there is capital flight, because dollar debt service strongly contributes to the continuation of exchange crises that make it profitable to hold dollars. If convertibility were suspended for creditors, the imminence of currency collapse (both in the exchange market and on the inflation front) would be reduced. As a result, capital would begin to return. The return of capital that has flown would ultimately sustain a long-term, orderly service of the debt, along with economic reconstruction of the debtor economies.

[16] *These points are developed at length in Dornbusch (1988a, 1988b).*

CONCLUSION

Latin America's disastrous economic performance in the 1980s is in large measure the result of capital flight. Capital flight is, of course, only the proximate cause. On the domestic side, the immediate causes are poor public finance and the ever-recurring temptation to sustain disequilibrium real exchange rates. On the external side, commodity and debt shocks contributed their share to worsening budgets and making exchange rates unrealistic.

The contrast between Asia and Latin America is striking: Asia did have many of the same shocks, but capital flight was never allowed to become a major issue. In large measure Asia's superior performance reflects more responsible fiscal policies and a more careful approach to exchange rates. But it may also reflect to some extent a very different income distribution.

Clearly, capital mobility is a basic reality for Latin America today, and when it comes into play it imposes major burdens on the economy. Capital is mobile, but labor is not. Capital flight is a resource transfer abroad (on account of *some* domestic residents). These transfers are ultimately achieved at the cost of lower real wages and lower growth in the standards of living of those who cannot move. Capital flight is basically unstoppable—there is no really successful instance of capital control—and the appropriate conclusion is that policies therefore must adapt in order to present less cause and opportunity for capital flight.

APPENDIX A

Modeling the Capital Flight Motive

In principle, there are four separate motivations for capital flight: 1) expected devaluation, 2) politics, 3) financial repression and missing markets, and 4) tax considerations. In reality, these motives tend to overlap for any individual country, with different considerations being paramount at different times. The basic portfolio problem, stated in terms of a choice between domestic and "foreign" (by denomination and possibly location) investment, involves a comparison of rates of return. Let i be the expected after-tax return on a domestic asset; i*, the after tax return abroad; and x, the expected rate of depreciation of the home (that is, the developing country's) currency. For a risk-neutral investor, foreign assets will be more attractive than home assets if the expected return from tax evasion and expected depreciation exceeds the home after-tax rate of return, or if

(1) $$(1+i^*)(1+x) > (1+i)(1-t)$$

or alternatively, in terms of real rates of return, if

(la) $$(1+r^*)(1+\delta) > (1+r)(1-t),$$

where δ is the expected rate of change of the real exchange rate and t is the marginal tax rate in the home country.

The criterion in (la) shows that with anticipated real depreciation, capital will move abroad unless home real interest rates exceed those abroad. The expected depreciation is especially important in the context of overvaluation situations. When it is widely perceived that a maxi-depreciation lies ahead, capital flight will become massive.

This is especially the case when capital movements can take place freely at the official exchange rate. This was, in fact, the case in Argentina and Mexico during several overvaluation episodes. An attempt to postpone exchange rate adjustment then implies large reserve losses (typically financed by borrowing abroad).

Criterion (la) above assumes that investors are risk neutral and evaluate investments by expected return. If investors are risk averse, then diversification considerations also influence portfolio choices. A potentially more important problem is determination of the expected return on foreign assets. This involves a judgment of how sustainable the government's exchange rate program is. We sketch here the bare bones of such a model.

The "speculative attacks" literature has arisen out of the study of these experiences. Lizondo (1983), in an influential article, showed that the Mexican forward rates invariably showed an expectation of a depreciation, even when the exchange rate was fixed. The expectation was, of course, borne out by subsequent events. Krugman (1979) and Connolly (1986) are examples of models of speculative attack. In capital markets, maturities for loans shrink, and the high nominal interest rates required to stem capital flight crowd out productive investment and may imply a rapid accumulation of domestic debts, often followed by bankruptcy.

Let us briefly consider a model of the external balance and the interest rate/ exchange rate trade-off a government must sustain to avoid capital flight. Let us suppose that the typical investor considers an exchange rate collapse to be probable. We can denote net disbursements of foreign exchange by F:[17]

$$F = x - \alpha\varphi + \beta\,\delta, \tag{2}$$

where x is a random disturbance to the current account, φ is the real exchange rate, and δ is the expected return differential on foreign assets.

$$\begin{aligned}\delta &= (1-p)i^* + p(i^*+\Delta) - i \\ &= i^*-i + p\Delta,\end{aligned} \tag{3}$$

where i and i^* are the home and foreign interest rates, p is the probability of a program failure, and Δ is the capital gain on foreign assets in case of a program failure. Substituting (3) into (2), we obtain

$$F = x - \alpha\varphi + \beta(i^*-i + p\Delta) \tag{4}$$

Note from (4) that the net foreign exchange disbursements themselves, via capital flight, depend on the probability of a program failure. The higher the probability of devaluation, the larger is capital flight and hence net disbursements.

The model is closed by a model of program failure. The probability of an exchange rate collapse is the probability that net exchange disbursements exceed the reserves of the authorities, R:

$$p = p(x+ \beta\delta - \alpha\varphi > R) \tag{5}$$

To estimate this probability we need to make an assumption about the distribution of x. But in general we can write the probability of program failure

[17] *We can think here of a one-shot game so that the stock flow distinction does not apply. Accordingly, net foreign exchange disbursements measure the loss of reserves from trade transactions and capital flows.*

as a function of the structural parameters, the distribution parameters, interest differentials, and reserves:[18]

$$(6) \qquad \begin{aligned} p &= p(i-i^*, \varphi, R, \beta, \Delta, \sigma^2) \\ P_1, P_2, P_3 &< 0 \\ P_4, P_5, P_6 &> 0 \end{aligned}$$

where σ^2 is the variance of x. This model implies that the probability of program failure, and hence of the capital flight that helps bring it about, is smaller

- the higher the initial reserves, R
- the more undervalued the real exchange rate (higher φ)
- the less responsive capital flight is to the expected yield differential as measured by the parameter ß
- the higher home relative to foreign interest rates, i-i*
- the smaller the capital gain on foreign assets in case of devaluation, Δ
- the less volatile trade flows as measured by the variance σ^2.

The model thus makes the point that the authorities can directly influence capital flight by targeting those variables that have a bearing on the probability of devaluation, specifically the interest differential and the level of the real exchange rate. These concerns are more important the lower the level of reserves relative to random swings in trade flows.

The government can stem capital flight by a combination of high interest rates and a very competitive real exchange rate. One thing it cannot do is have a real exchange rate that is unlikely to balance the current account *and* an interest differential that does not favor the home country. In that case, capital flight is inevitable, and a breakdown of the exchange rate regime is virtually certain.

[18] *See Dornbusch (1989) for a detailed discussion of these results.*

APPENDIX B

This appendix updates the capital flight estimates reported in Cumby and Levich (1987). The following definitions are used:

A = Current account surplus
B = Net foreign direct investment
C = Private short-term capital inflows
D = Portfolio investment (bonds and equities)
E = Banking system foreign assets (- signifies increase)
F = Change in reserves (- signifies increase)
G = Errors and omissions
H = Change in (gross) debt

Cumby and Levich report various measures of capital flight. We report here an update on three of these. The measures of capital flight are as follows:

A+B+F+H World Bank, Erbe
A+B+E+F+H Morgan Guaranty
G+C Cuddington

Table A.1. Latin America: Alternative Measures of Capital Flight (1983-1987)
(Billions of U.S. dollars)

Country	Method		
	World Bank, Erbe	Morgan Guaranty	Cuddington
Argentina	6.8	6.2	0.4
Brazil	24.6	23.2	7.0
Mexico	35.3	34.0	17.6
Peru	3.3	3.3	2.0
Venezuela	18.8	18.4	6.2

BIBLIOGRAPHY

Alarco, Germán, et al. (1985). *La Dolarización y su Impacto en la Economía Peruana.* Lima: Fundación Friedrich Ebert.

Alexander, L. (1987). "Debt Conversions: Economic Issues for Heavily Indebted Developing Countries." International Finance Discussion Papers No. 315. Board of Governors of the Federal Reserve.

Bernstein, M., ed. (1966). *Foreign Investment in Latin America.* New York: Alfred A. Knopf, Inc.

Bhagwati, J., and A. Krueger (1974). "Capital Flight from LDCs: A Statistical Analysis." In J. Bhagwati (ed.), *Illegal Transactions in International Trade,* Amsterdam: North Holland.

Blanco, E., and P. Garber (1986). "Recurrent Devaluation and Speculative Attacks on the Mexican Peso." *Journal of Political Economy* 94, 1: 148-166.

Brown, B. (1987). *The Flight of International Capital.* London: Croom Helm.

Cardoso, E., and R. Dornbusch (1988). "Private Capital for Economic Development." In H. Chenery and T.N. Srinivasan (eds.), *Handbook of Economic Development,* Amsterdam: North Holland.

Conesa, E. (1986). "The Causes of Capital Flight from Latin America." Mimeo. Inter-American Development Bank.

Connolly, M. (1986). "The Speculative Attack on the Peso and the Real Exchange Rate: Argentina 1981." *Journal of International Money and Finance* 5 (March): 117-130.

Cuddington, J. (1986). *Capital Flight: Estimates, Issues, and Explanations.* Princeton Studies in International Finance 58. Princeton: Princeton University.

........(1987). "Macroeconomic Determinants of Capital Flight. An Econometric Investigation." In D. Lessard and John J. Williamson (eds.), *Capital Flight: The Problem and Policy Responses,* Washington, D.C.: Institute for International Economics.

Cumby, R., and R. Levich (1987). "On the Definition and Magnitude of Recent Capital Flight." In D. Lessard and John J. Williamson (eds.), *Capital Flight: The Problem and Policy Responses,* Washington, D.C.: Institute for International Economics.

Deppler, M., and M. Williamson (1987). "Capital Flight: Concepts, Measurement, and Issues." In *Staff Studies for the World Economic Outlook,* Washington, D.C.: International Monetary Fund (August).

Dooley, M. (1986). "Country-Specific Risk Premiums, Capital Flight and Net Investment Income Payments in Selected Developing Countries." Unpublished. International Monetary Fund (March).

........(1986). "Capital Flight: A Response to Differences in Financial Risk." Mimeo. International Monetary Fund.

Dornbusch, R. (1985). "External Debt, Budget Deficits, and Disequilibrium Exchange Rates." In G. Smith and J. Cuddington (eds.), *International Debt and the Developing Countries*, Washington, D.C.: World Bank.

........(1987a). "Capital Flight and Misinvoicing: Motives, Evidence and Macroeconomic Implications." Mimeo. Massachusetts Institute of Technology.

........(1988a). Background Paper to the Twentieth Century Task Force Report *The Road To Recovery*. New York: Twentieth Century Fund.

........(1988b). "Mexico: Stabilization and Growth." *Economic Policy* 2.

........(1989). "A Positive Theory of Credibility in Stabilization." Mimeo. Massachusetts Institute of Technology.

........and J.C. de Pablo (1988). *Argentina: Debt and Macroeconomic Problems*. Mimeo. Massachusetts Institute of Technology. (A Spanish version has been published by SudAmericana, Buenos Aires).

Eaton, J. (1987a). "Public Capital for Economic Development." In H. Chenery and T.N. Srinivasan (eds.), *Handbook of Economic Development*, Vol. II.

........(1987b). "Public Debt Guarantees and Private Capital Flight." *World Bank Economic Review* I, 3: 377-395.

Edwards, S. (1986). "Order of Liberalization of the Current and Capital Account of the Balance of Payments." In A. Choksi and D. Papageorgiou (eds.), *Economic Liberalization in Developing Countries*, Oxford: Basil Blackwell.

El-Erian, M. (1988). "Currency Substitution in Egypt and the Yemen Arab Republic." IMF *Staff Papers*, Vol. 35 (March): 85-103.

Erbe, S. (1985). "The Flight of Capital from Developing Countries." *Intereconomics* 20 (November): 268-275.

Fernández, R. (1985). "The Expectations Management Approach to Stabilization in Argentina: 1976-82." *World Development* 13 (August): 871-892.

Feuerlein, W., and E. Hannan (1940). *Dollars in Latin America.* New York: Council on Foreign Relations.

Fischer, S. (1982). "Seigniorage and the Case for a National Money." *Journal of Political Economy* (April).

Flood, R., and P. Garber (1984). "Collapsing Exchange Rate Regimes." *Journal of International Economics* 17, No. 1/2: 1-13.

Gordon, D., and R. Levine (1988). "The Capital Flight Problem." International Finance Discussion Papers 320. Board of Governors of the Federal Reserve (April).

Gulati, S. (1987). "A Note on Trade Misinvoicing." In D. Lessard and J. Williamson (eds.), *Capital Flight and Third World Debt*, Washington, D.C.: Institute for International Economics.

Hale, D. D. (1987). "The Economic Case for Encouraging Greater Foreign Participation in Third World Equity Markets." Mimeo. Chicago: Kemper Financial Services, Inc.

Henry, J. (1986). "Where the Money Went." *The New Republic* (April 14).

Isze, A., and G. Ortiz (1987). "Fiscal Rigidities, Public Debt and Capital Flight." IMF *Staff Papers* 34, No. 2 (June): 311-332.

Kahkonen, J. (1987). "Liberalization Policies and Welfare in a Financially Repressed Economy." IMF *Staff Papers* 34, (September): 531-547.

Khan, M., and N. Ul Haque (1985). "Foreign Borrowing and Capital Flight: A Formal Analysis." IMF *Staff Papers* 32 (December): 606-628.

Krugman, P. (1979). "A Model of Balance of Payments Crises." *Journal of Money, Credit and Banking* 11, 3 (August): 311-325.

Lessard, D., and J. Williamson (1987). "The Problem and Policy Responses." In D. Lessard and J. Williamson (eds.), *Capital Flight and Third World Debt,* Washington, D.C.: Institute for International Economics.

Lizondo, S. (1983). "Foreign Exchange Futures Prices under Fixed Exchange Rates." *Journal of International Economics* 14, No. 1-2:69-84.

Maddala, G.S. (1977). *Econometrics.* New York: McGraw-Hill.

Márquez, J. (1987). "Money Demand in Open Economies: A Currency Substitution Model of Venezuela." *Journal of International Money and Finance* 6, 2 (June): 167-178.

Morgan Guaranty Trust Company (1986). *World Financial Markets* (March and September). New York.

Nurkse, R. *International Currency Experience in the Interwar Period.* Geneva: League of Nations.

Ortiz, G. (1983). "Dollarization in Mexico: Causes and Consequences." In P. Aspe et al. (eds.), *Financial Policies and the World Capital Market: The Case of Latin America,* Chicago: University of Chicago Press.

Poloz, S. (1986). "Currency Substitution and the Precautionary Demand for Money." *Journal of International Money and Finance* 5 (March): 115-124.

Ramírez-Rojas, C. (1985). "Currency Substitution in Argentina, Mexico and Uruguay." IMF *Staff Papers* 32 (December): 629-667.

Reynoso, A. (1988a). "When Financial Regulation Becomes Financial Repression: The Case of Mexico (1940-1982)." Mimeo. Massachusetts Institute of Technology.

........(1988b). "Capital Flight and Missing Markets: Mexico in 1982." Mimeo. Massachusetts Institute of Technology.

Rodríguez, C.A. (1982). "The Argentine Stabilization Plan of December 20th." *World Development* 10, 9: 801-811.

Rodríguez, M.A. (1987). "Consequences of Capital Flight for Latin America." In D. Lessard and J. Williamson (eds.), *Capital Flight and Third World Debt,* Washington, D.C.: Institute for International Economics.

Solis, L., and L. Zedillo (1985). "The Foreign Debt of Mexico." In G. Smith and J. Cuddington (eds.), *International Debt and the Developing Countries,* Washington, D.C.: World Bank.

Tornell, A. (1988). "Irreversible Real Capital, Reversible Financial Capital and Welfare-Improving Tobin Taxes." Mimeo. New York: Columbia University.

United Nations (1949). *International Capital Movements during the Interwar Period*. New York.

........(1954). *The International Flow of Private Capital 1946-52.* New York.

........(1965). *External Financing in Latin America.* New York.

Wallich, H. (1943). "The Future of Latin American Dollar Bonds." *Economic Review* 43, 2 (June): 321-335.

Walter, I. (1985). *Secret Money.* Lexington, Mass.: Lexington Books.

Zedillo, E. (1985). "The Mexican External Debt: The Last Decade." In M. Wionczek (ed.), *Politics and Economics of the External Debt Crisis,* Boulder: Westview Press.

Rudiger Dornbusch, currently a Ford International Professor of Economics at MIT, has made a significant contribution to the field of international economics through extensive writing and active participation in organizations such as the National Bureau of Economic Research (NBER), the Brookings Panel on Economic Activity, and the American Economic Association.

In addition to serving as assistant editor of the Quarterly Journal of Economics *and the* Journal of International Economics, *Mr. Dornbusch has recently written books on exchange rates, inflation, and the external debt.*